THE COLOURS OF MY MIND

Coco Schreiber

ARTHUR H. STOCKWELL LTD
Torrs Park, Ilfracombe, Devon, EX34 8BA
Established 1898
www.ahstockwell.co.uk

© *Coco Schreiber, 2021*
First published in Great Britain, 2021

The moral rights of the author have been asserted.

*All rights reserved.
No part of this publication may be reproduced
or transmitted in any form or by any means,
electronic or mechanical, including photocopy,
recording, or any information storage and
retrieval system, without permission
in writing from the copyright holder.*

*British Library Cataloguing-in-Publication Data.
A catalogue record for this book is available
from the British Library.*

DEDICATION

To those I've loved . . .
and lost . . .
or perhaps just mislaid.

ISBN 978-0-7223-5107-9
*Printed in Great Britain by
Arthur H. Stockwell Ltd
Torrs Park   Ilfracombe
Devon   EX34 8BA*

CONTENTS

BLUE WAVES

On Sappho's Isle	5
J'Adore, J'Adore	6
Sherbet Fountains	7
Amazonian	8
Of Passion	9
Who Knows?	10
Arrhythmic	12
In the Potting Shed	13
Late Home	14
Commitment	15
Satin Moon (or Florentine Magic)	16
Given	18
Paris	19

ON SAPPHO'S ISLE

Steamy hot afternoon air.
Open windows.
The dishevelled bedsheets greedily wrap their
twisted lengths around our naked forms.

Exhausted now – ribcage rises and falls out of sync
with heartbeat, the one free arm pulses full length
against a pillow, but softly.

Head turns inward and rests against Lovely's breast;
hand cups its rounded fullness so strokingly gently
and urges the firming strawberry top to her lips,
expressing it carefully, sucking it dry.

Knees slide over, hooking on, bodies now falling, one on one.
Exploring hands pursue their curious investigation
and drown in the warm depths of their goal.

J'ADORE, J'ADORE

Can't go on like this – must stop thinking of you, miles away.
I need distraction: shops, shops.
Mustn't go in there – the all-enveloping net of your
perfume encircles my senses – I see its name writ
large in lighted signs – it suffocates me, deliciously.

Would that I could be there with you, spread over
your body, smothering your pulsating so-tender
spots, yearning for me to kiss them dry, perfume
lingering in the air, two being one.

SHERBET FOUNTAINS

Arching backs, supple as never were, now bendy as willow wands moving to the caressing motion of strong hands bringing slumbering emotions to life in a hail of sherbet showers.

The calling of her name in breathy tones at the very peak of crisis, the eventual slackening as we give way to release and curious, quivering calm.

AMAZONIAN

Immeasurable length of leg sauntered forward cutting a wake through the shallow surf; no splash of water, no break of wave, just soundless progress towards the waiting object of her irrepressible need.

With sun baking sand and salt across her back, silhouetting her frame as she halted in front of the other woman, the Amazon goddess peeled off her skin-tight shirt, exposing the very obvious details of her torso, standing prouder than before, anticipating the trembling touch of the so-named handmaiden.

Then without a word, a sound, she was gone.

All that was left was the skin-tight shirt. . . .

OF PASSION

The measured heaving of controlled lungs
    within expanding cage;
        the puckered brow glistens with shimmering
        sweatlets about to drizzle down her cheeks
        as she gives herself wholly to the all-smothering
        cushion of Love's pulsating kiss, lips closing
        in over her half-smiling mouth.

Tongues touch, tentatively – half-resisting, not
    pushing forward, then urging onward ever
    so slightly.
    Love's lips dab teasingly at her open
    invitation, her moistened tongue slides over
    her teeth, carefully, always carefully, always
    gently, always hesitatingly.
    This gentle being must not be hurt by a
    passion so hot that a volcano would yield.

The head rolls back, the throat gives way to
    Love's massaging lips, while hands en-cup
    each yielding breast, vibrating at the unsubtle
    cry that erupts from the soul.

WHO KNOWS?

Can they tell?
Fellow shoppers – neighbours.
Can they tell?
Mutual friends – colleagues.
Can they tell?
Family – anyone.

Do I care?
They don't care.
They don't suspect.
They don't know.
They don't believe.
Would she dare?

She's drinking more!
How d'you know – are you always there?
She's smiling more – more than before.
Secret smile, like Mona Lisa. . . .
She was always weird. . . .
Don't care, d'you?

Can they tell?
Can they hear my heartbeat quicken?
Do they know why my arms are folded in front of
my chest?
Can they tell why my face has the amplified colour
chart of overripe tomatoes?
Can they tell?
Can they?

Someone at the door:
it's her.
Let her in –
no, don't – please.
I can't stand it.
Door opens. . . .

And there she stands – magnificent, brazen.
I've turned to mush: squillions of volcanoes have
exploded within me.
My overripe tomato face has faded to a pale
parsnip hue, and my lips don't stop quivering until
she has my face in her hands, pressing it to her
mouth.

Now they DO have something to talk about.

NOW they can tell. . . .

ARRHYTHMIC

The day didn't start well –
    the car didn't start at all;
    the buses aren't running;
    the trains are on strike!
    My bicycle has a flat tyre –
    the pump's in the shed –
    I dropped and lost the key to the thing when
we fell out of bed.

This can't be love.

My satin pyjamas are patterned with toothpaste;
my new pale-blue shirt's got a stain:
it happened last night when I tripped near the
compost – and the beetroot soup
    boiled over again.

Surely this can't be anything at all whatsoever to
do with love!

I dream of her daily, in every minute;
nights apart are much worse – lonelier.
I need to feel her breathing life into the world,
into the space that surrounds me;
she is my life, my everything.

Could THIS be love?

I know I need her.
I know I trust her.
I know I adore her.
I know I want her.

If this is Love, I'm in it.

IN THE POTTING SHED

She took in a deep reviving breath as she
   opened the potting-shed door;
   it smelt of earth, it smelt of earth-water, it
   smelt of . . . her.

Just.

Sun stroked the glass with searching fingers
   of light;
   silent particles of dust swam in the
   hovering streams of the expanding
   warmth.

Healing.

Words that should never have been uttered
   gripped long-redundant vine tentacles;
   stubborn, unmeant, hurtful.

Killing.

She stood at the window and cried her name
   time and time again.
   She crumpled, clung on to the bench, emotion
   weakening her legs, despair overtaking her.

Until: arms encirled her waist and halted
   her downward slide.
   She gripped the hands and leant back.
   "No more, no more" came the words to
   her ear.

Secure.

LATE HOME

I knew she'd be late –
    she said she might be;
    I heard the front door open
    and close.
I pulled the blanket up to my
    chin, then pulled it down
    again in case fluff got up my
    nose!

She greeted our dog and swore at the
    cat –
    I knew all was well after that;
she called out my name, and then
    again as she quietly came up
    the stairs.

She sat on the bed and slipped off
    her shoes, which clattered on the
    oak floor;
she pulled at my earlobe, and
    whispered my name, which inflamed
    my desires to the core!

COMMITMENT

The ring you carried with you all that
    time:
        turquoise as the seas that took you
        away – and that brought you back to me.
That ring now adorns my hand, as we both
    wanted, hidden in plain sight.

Let us lie together and commit Love!

The gentle seas and sands enwrap us in
    their caressing warmth, holding us
    tenderly in their familiar embrace,
    protecting from the intermittent
    harshness of life.

Let us be bound together and commit
    Love.

It is my greatest hope that we stay
    as one;
        that we float together on those
        turquoise seas.

Let me spread myself over you and
    commit Love.

SATIN MOON
(or Florentine Magic)

The city's singing bells disturb the
    quiet;
       its maddening weekend traffic
    stops at last.
The stifling layers of heat are steadily
    rising from the street
    up to the rooftops, then the
    mountains in the air.

Our house, a veritable palace in a row
    of ancient villas,
       greets us warmly as we enter, hand
    in hand;
we walk the several landings to the floors
    above the streets and resolve there
    to remain until the morn!

Our bedroom in the clouds boasts a bed
    of wild proportions;
       the claret satin sheets call out to us;
       the heavy velvet curtains reach the
    ceiling and its stars,
       and the moonlight bathes the bed
    in streaks of gold.

We lie side by side, naturally adorned, on
the cool moon-soaked sheets, legs
entwined;
the soft satin covers caress us, as lovers,
to reach our conclusion, well defined.

There's a little bit of loss once the crisis
is released,
once the damning of emotions has been
breached;
there is crying, there is craving, there is
weeping, there is calling, there is magic
in the whisper of a name.

GIVEN

Your eyes:
    deep, deep wells of secret wantings.

Your hands:
    soft cups cushioning these tender,
    yielding breasts – yearning.
    Calling.
    Silently.

Your voice:
    alto, breathy, coaxing, slipping into
    my mind, calming my anxious moment.

Take.

Me.

PARIS

And there I stood by the crying-bed:
untidy, unstill, unquiet, unwarm –
deceived by untruthful breath.

"I'll love you forever. I'll leave you
never. To you only can I be true.
I always did love you, and always
shall need you."

You look at me and I fall into your
eyes:
with a lie on your lips, with a
dart in my heart,
watch as I drown . . .
in . . .
you. . . .

CONTENTS

PURPLE MISTS

Foreign Travel	22
Midnight Feast	23
At the Party	24
Let's Have a Little Drinky	26
R. U?	27

FOREIGN TRAVEL

The unfamiliar train station, dark and smokey –
   foreign smokey –
   uninviting.

Door stood open, I thought:
   soon attained life and slammed
   into me in a swift backwards
   movement.

I swore.
   Silly little English leather suitcase,
   pre-war, positioned itself before
   my right foot;
   I tripped, and stood on it with
   my left.

I swore again.
   I could almost hear the cheese
   and tomatoes melding into the
   bread: the sandwiches I'd made
   myself hours earlier.

Sat at a small table, bit of a mistake:
   kitchen door was flung open, slammed
   against my head;
   it closed to reveal my nice new straw
   hat, over-brimmed, repositioned
   over left eye, and soup spoon
   standing proudly between my breasts
   like a flagpole.

I sighed, slammed my elbow down right
   into the middle of a freshly buttered
   bread roll.

MIDNIGHT FEAST

We shivered in the dorm at night –
   not the warmest place on earth;
   bedsocks and bottles, coffee, chocolate,
   bikkies by candlelight.

School run like clockwork, military
   precision;
   refectory smelt of burning most days;
   bubble and squeak and hide and seek,
   the under-cooks suffered derision.

Back in the dorm we gathered in tents:
   huge blankets we'd tied over bedposts.
   We snuggled together and pooled our
   resources and dished out digestives
   and mints.

Ladies from upper sixth valued their army,
   did Coral and Dulcie and Steph'nie;
   out from the floorboards and secret
   wall-chambers came treasures of
   choc'late and everything any self-
   respecting schoolgirl could ever have
   dreamed of in the confines of the
   school's dorm in deep midwinter by
   the river.

At midnight.

AT THE PARTY

That first glance, the slight flicker of
    a smile flashed around your lips for
    a split second.
That was all.
No more.

You resumed your accustomed poise
    and returned to your group two
    tables away as before . . .
    but with one slight change:
    you angled yourself differently, abetting
    an uninterrupted view across the
    room – to me!

I feigned disinterest, focused on the
    band.
Elbow resting on table's edge, I raised
    my glass mouthwards, but before
    being able to sip of the fizz-full
    nectar my elbow and the table severed
    company and my décolletage was
    baptised with Italy's favourite
    go-to tipple.

I was mortified – and wet – and suddenly
    I became the sole focus of attention
    of *that* table.
Some of the kind ladies rushed over
    with paper napkins and dabbed
    me dry.

I was now embarrassed AND wet, and having been assured that I was fine they went back to their party.
I thought I was alone.
I was wrong.
I tried to move my chair, intending to make a dash for the door, and freedom, but the chair was immoveable.
Stuck.

You've guessed it: the woman with the enigmatic smile was holding on to it, trapping me.
"You're not running?" she asked.
"Aren't I?" I stammered.
"No!" She took my hand and led me towards the party table, and introductions were made.

I explained that I didn't have the courage of a gnat, or the g-guts of a g-nu, and just wanted to escape!

In the end it turned out to be an enjoyable evening – and still is, so many years on.

LET'S HAVE LITTLE DRINKY

From Sekt to Prosecco,
    from champagne to fizz:
    to thinkers it's all much the same!
    From headache to toothache,
    from backache to heartache, to
    lovers it's all the same game.

We dress to impress;
We disarm her with charm,
    and commit to eternal endeavour to
    play by the rules and be treated
    as fools and stay locked in
    confusion for ever.

It's dry when it rains;
It's loss when it's gain;
It's always when really it's never;
It's cold when it's hot, and you freeze
    to the spot, and you're locked in
    confusion for ever.

You're frightened and nauseous,
    disinterested, curious,
    lost in the game to deceive her.
She fooled you aplenty –
    she's not complimentary;
    you're locked in confusion for ever.

R. U?

I've known them fattish,
I've known them thinnish,
I've known them in-betweenish;
I've known them Welshish, even Scottish,
   also English-ish-ish-ish-ish.

I've known 'em clever, known 'em brainy,
   with a keen artistic leaning,
   with a love of dogs and cats (though
   not at home).
I've known 'em cunning and deceitful,
   loving – and a handful!
But are you the one I've found for me alone?

CONTENTS

YELLOW CUSHIONS

Prose and Prosecco (or Self-Medication)	30
Nonpareil	31
In Grace	32
In the Old Garden	33
This Rover's Not for Turning	34
In a Medieval Garden	35
Where Is the World?	36
Return	37
A Sprint, Not a Marathon	38
Like an Icenean Torc	39

PROSE AND PROSECCO
(or Self-Medication)

You see, I'm an unsocial bod;
I do not crave the company of humans.
The thought of selfish, screaming, moaning,
    sticky-runny-nosed under-forties does
    nothing but enhance, to the nth degree,
    my total adoration of THE DOG.

Pause for Prosecco.

I lie abed, be it day or night, and luxuriate in
    the pitter-patter of paws around my home.
Muddied carpets do not infuriate, nor the
    toe-cracking remnants of a bone.

Pause for Prosecco.

The cracks in the windows and the gaps round
    the doors allow freezing gales good access;
fresh air's important – a vital component – when
    a country dog you try to impress.

Pause for Prosecco.

Obfuscation surrounds our fight for the armchair:
    how did I end up on the floor!
In my flight through the air I flew over the chair,
    and my head hit the top of the door!

Pause for Pawsecco.

NONPAREIL

In my shameless attempt to instruct with contempt
the pastime of full inebriety,
I have, nonetheless, and with somewhat success,
forsaken my place in society.

The ladies and lords tend to gather in hordes,
and partake of a tipple or eight;
they swing their legs over dear Dobbin and Clover,
then find they just sat on the gate!

With perfect precision, guffaws of derision
are flung at their muddied demeanours;
the ladies in top hats, in black skirts and white spats,
resume talk of old Argentina.

The gentlemen there do not give of a care
when a lady refuses a hand-up:
she grabs at his chaps, which he's tied to the back
of his donkey who's called Alejandro*.

* ALEHANDRO

IN GRACE

A light, refreshingly airy path along the
edge of the copse sees the copsewood
parting its length to guide you, my
lovely, along its dried but narrow
footway.

Tall, supple saplings bow with grace as you
pass, acknowledging your courtesy as
you step carefully between the dear wild
flowers of the season, and they, smiling,
disperse their sweetly perfumed pollens
toward you on the gentle, zephyrous
airwaves.

The balmy forenoon, the copse's most
treasured time, cushions the wild sweet briar
and heady eglantine as they shelter from
the harsh midday beams of Will's 'eye
of heaven'.

IN THE OLD GARDEN

An unquiet path commits the curious
   walker softly and unremarkably along
   and down its length, the sand-coloured
   gravel murmuring like steps on
   cornflakes.

An unhurried left turn at the old oak opens
   up an unexpected vista over the
   valley below: tissue-thin slivers of
   silver-pink mist float between and
   above the immature hillocks.

The curious walker halts her perambulation
   involuntarily and catches her breath
   with a surprise-laden "Oh-h!"
   The sight is such that superlatives
   evade her as she kneels and surveys
   the ever changing scene.

Sun soon emerges and melts the chiffon
   scarves, and with a burst of sun-spray
   an observant blackbird flies down and
   pecks at the ground, annoying the
   squirrels at the curious walker's feet.

Close-cupped buds on skeletal-branched
   shrubs begin to burst forth from their
   green jackets, and yawning dormice,
   newly awoken from months abed,
   discover a healthy appetite!

THIS ROVER'S NOT FOR TURNING

I am not 'factured as other gels –
I do not crave the hourglass bod,
    but must be happy and content with
    what I've got:
    I have height, I have depth, not
    inclined to indecision,
    but with numbers, never words, I am
    inept.

My roving eye conspires to rove a trifle
    wider than the hills and vales
    I've roved thus far to find
    the shapely leg a-welded to
    a bod of fine proportions –
    or a head of dreams transfixéd in
    the skies.

IN A MEDIEVAL GARDEN

Eyes like stars pause, entranced, before
    the panoply of tones and textures of
    myriad plantlets displayed on glasshouse
    tables.

Buss me, my lady.

Gentle myosotis, small but regal violets,
    cushioning primrose;
    the spiky columbine, as yet soft, but
    hiding its pointy spears neath
    leafy pillows.

Buss me, my lovely.

A walk along the rose-way: those regal
    princesses, enthroned, hold crownéd
    bud-heads high above the masses, soon
    to show their allegiances to royal
    ancestry.

Buss me. Buss me. Buss me.

WHERE IS THE WORLD?

A perfect cadence seemed to bring to an
 absolute end the glorious chorus of
 birdsong that morning – or perhaps it
 was the shifting key change in the
 breeze's harmonic direction!

The emotive piccolo-like hard 'ticking',
 fast-moving trill of the darling little
 wren ended with a tremble through
 her whole diminutive body.
 She is protective of her domain, but
 not isolationist, enjoying group hugs
 on wintry nights!

The robin, our national favourite,
 warbles melodiously in spring, but
 in autumn moves, andante, into a
 minor key.

How sad that so many of us fail to notice
 such natural visual and audible diversity
 in this land of ours!
How can the cuckoo go unnoticed in
 spring?

Why are the gulls noticed only when they
 thieve chips from man-loved
 plastic boxes!

Where is it gone, this world that was?

   Open your eyes and look –

   Open your ears and listen –

   Open your heart and . . .

      be.

RETURN

Absence is ache, not pain;
    it is an emptiness, an emptiness,
    but filled with a longing for, it is
    a tugging, a pulling feeling into
    the solar plexus – that network
    of nerves.

It can be felt within a minute of you
    leaving – or an hour, or a day,
    Or a split second.
    Cannot be seen, only felt.

There is an impalpable link between
    the mind and the physical body.
That link can be made whole only when
    you return.
The second we are together the chain is
    renewed, is strong.

Mouth on mouth.
Hand cupping breast.
Legs entwining;
Together supportive, embracing, loving.

As . . .
    One . . .
        Again.

A SPRINT, NOT A MARATHON

The unimplied goal was a dead heat – it
   had to be; anything else would have
   seemed contrived.
The two mounts moved around each
   other taking mental notes, planning
   a strategy, pacing.
The blink of an eye and the game was on.
The pace was unremarkable at first:
   searching, almost; teasing, certainly;
   questioning, too.

The intensity increased with the pace, but
   was still comfortable,
   until the pace was faster, the pressure,
   harder –
   faster and harder –
   faster and harder,
      then explosive,
         and both mounts called out and
      fell together, eyes each on the other.

LIKE AN ICENEAN TORC

The cutting calls from the local air
    station's wheezing silver eagles
    pierce the sweating air hovering
    around our room as they slice
    through Byron's beautifully blue
    sky.

I raise myself up on wobbly elbow and
    glance down to you, your smiling
    mouth, tremulous.

Beckoning.

Our lips melt together.

Delicious.

Arms, legs swirl round like an Icenean
    torc.

Bodies relax in each other. Hearts pound
    tutti.

Sleep provides a welcome coverlet on
    a bed of eider's down.

CONTENTS

GREY PATHS

Sacrifice 42

SACRIFICE

. . . . and suddenly I saw the end approaching.
Nothing of note had happened.
And everything.
Feelings didn't lessen – quite the opposite.
Perhaps that was the problem, if there
    was one.
It was all so intense, right from the start,
    but it was all so genuine, on both sides.
    And, I suspect, still is.

"You two love too much. You're almost on
    fire with it. Remember, fire consumes!"
    this mutual friend intoned to us one
    visit.

I didn't want my presence to be the raison
    d'être for the disintegration of her private
    family – or, indeed, of her public life.
I shall step away completely until really needed
    again – if ever.
We'll miss so much – we both know this.
It's genuinely for the best.

Mutual friend asked, "Won't you miss the physical
    side as well as the day-to-day?"
And kindly, almost as an aside, 'How was the sex?'

Es war astronomisch.

CONTENTS

RED ROSES

I Remember the Cottage by the Sea (1)	44
I Remember the Cottage by the Sea (2)	46
I Remember the Cottage by the Sea (3)	47
I Remember the Cottage by the Sea (4)	48

I REMEMBER THE COTTAGE BY THE SEA (1)

In my mind's eye I see the large garden by the sea, the small child clutching Great-Grand-Dam's hand, the white-bubble-haired head tilted up to the lady adoringly, the Great-Grand-Dam beaming tenderly, the black-and-white cat, well whiskered, was thus aptly named, an overzealous and highly successful mouser – as my mother, Great-Grand-Dam's granddaughter, would attest to after fishing out an offending rodent in her boot one immemorable day!

I remember the old kitchen, the large stone sinks, the perfectly uneven grey flagstones, the window, a massive glazed space in the wall above the sinks, affording a panoramic show of the large garden: the rows and rows and rows of sweet peas, mountaineering up and over stick-tents – Great-Grand-Dam would soon be picking their overlong perfumed stems to sell to the florist's on Lord Street, and buy impossible cream cakes (boxes thereof) at Madge Brewer's (confectioner), then trek back to the sea-cottage for afternoon tea.

Mid-mornings were fun – for me: sitting silently, obediently at the chunky kitchen table, and the top half of the door to the garden swung open, clattering, and a (to me) massive cow's head forced its way through, noisily followed by two others.
Great-Grand-Dam gave each bovine beauty a treat at their muzzles, whispered something to each one (I knew not what) and they in turn blew her a warming scented greeting as they backed out and sauntered towards the milking parlour across the lane a-front the cottage.

My then-three-year-old mind tries to pull me back there – alas, a journey possible only in the memory.

I REMEMBER THE COTTAGE BY THE SEA (2)

And down at the bottom of the garden,
    way past the sweet peas, lurked and
    glubbed the horrible, darkly pongy expanse
    of the ancient cesspool, now open to
    the clumsy clodden-footedness of one
    particularly clodden-footed aunt, sister and
    arch-enemy of my mother! That sister who
    was told to vacate the stage upon which
    she was dancing the role of a sweet, genteel
    sleeping princess, for noisily and over-
    enthusiastically chewing upon a large and
    very pink saliva-inducing mouthful of
    American chewing gum – thankfully,
    as it happens, not of the 'bubble' variety;
    that same sister walked backwards down
    the length of the garden, watching a group of
    visitors to my Great-Grand-Dam, turned
    round and walked straight into the cesspool.

I am told that this incident caused Great-Grand-
    Dam's timid black-and-white much be-
    whiskered cat to vacate the garden with some heretofore
    unobserved and unexpected turn of speed
    upon hardening toes and claws beneath
    curiously solidified and strangely stilt-like legs,
    the normally ground-scraping tail now as
    upright as a ship's boom. The
    corpse-enlivening screech proved of sufficient
    decibel-enriched power to alert the cottage
    sorority to the probability of a sudden demise.
    The ground-hugging flight of the feline Exocet
    indicated the direction of take-off, and therefore
    position of caterwauling aunt, who was
    eventually hauled inelegantly from the
    bowels of the acrid pit.

I REMEMBER THE COTTAGE BY THE SEA (3)

My enquiring mind had to ask about the eventual destination of the contents of the cesspool, and were they connected somehow with the lavatories in the curiously odoriferous shed at the top of the garden, not too far from the back door! The actual two lavatories were encased within a large wooden cabinet, ornately carved with what I used to think were creatures from Africa or outer space. (As I had never seen either at that time I decided they were both, and that I would never ever go to either place as the people who came from there appeared to have strange dangly bits in odd places which would clearly have made walking and riding most uncomfortable.)

My mother lost me one morning, claiming to have 'searched high and low for it'.
I appeared at the back door clutching Great-Grand-Dam's hand, grinning; my mother claimed again to have looked all over for me.
"You clearly don't know your daughter!" cooed Great-Grand-Dam.

How prophetic her words turned out to be!

I REMEMBER THE COTTAGE BY THE SEA
(4)

No mention was ever made, in my presence,
  of the terrifying cavalryman with the kindly,
  twinkling eyes who sat proudly astride
  a magnificent bestrapped and beribboned
  charger in the painting hanging above the
  fireplace in the forbidden confines of the
  'front parlour'.

If there had been a 'back parlour' I could never
  have found it on my illicit treks through
  the cottage. These adventures invariably
  ended with some adult triumphantly hauling
  me by the wrist, legs at full stretch
  still unable to reach the floor, all the way back
  to the kitchen, Mother chastising me, Grand-
  Dam joining in with all-too-apparent glee, and
  my champion, Great-Grand-Dam, winking
  at me knowingly, twinkling.

I never did find out about the cavalryman – but
  the women of the gathering were told, in
  no uncertain terms, not to chide me: "For
  'tis in her blood," cooed Great-Grand-Dam.
  They all drew their clasped hands up and
  under their well-protruding bosoms, at the
  same time sucking their teeth (those who
  had any) behind tightening lips. I am constantly
  bemused by the propensity of these certain
  women of a certain age of a certain
  social level within this matriarchy for the
  wearing
  of hats adorned with dead ducks.

Hasn't happened to me . . .
                              yet.